John Fox is an artist, print-maker, writer, cultural provocateur, occasional musician and poet. He lives in a wooden Beach House with a turf roof, above the shoreline of Morecambe Bay. This landscape permeates his work around radical notions of secular rites of passage, wilderness, vernacular art and gift relationships outside our commodity culture.

Published 2011 by Dead Good Guides
www.deadgoodguides.com

Copyright John Fox 2011

Illustrations by John Fox -
Drypoint etchings: *Cyclist* page 8
Captain page 101
Front cover painting: *Seaside Pier*

Photography by Duncan Copley

Layout and graphic elements provided by Blurb
Blurb are Blurb Inc. 2010

All rights reserved. No part of this book may be reproduced in any form or by any means without the written permission of the publisher

This book was created using the Blurb Creative Publishing Service

ISBN 978-0-9568583-1-3

You Never Know

a collection of poems
for occasions

John Fox

CONTENTS

Profane and Sacred

Gate	10
Half Moon Bay	12
Come in Noah	13
Washed Up	14
Superstore	15
Yellow Ducks	16
Getting Old	17
Farewell Party for Dr P	18
Urn	19

Funerals

The Age of Wisdom	23
Diz Willis	24
Midnight Mechanics	25
Bells	26
Max	27
Captain Fantastic	28
Five Poems for Boris	29
Arthur	31
Twelfth of May 2010	31
View	32
Waiting for the Light	32
Mermaids over Arran	33
In Memory of Val	34
For Adrian	36

A Question of Time

Hollow	40
On the Edge of a Heaving Tide	41
Frame Raising	43
A Question of Time	44
"The Ultimate Abode of the Just"	47
Lugworms	48
There will be Forever Herrings	49
Curlew	50
Nana's Dance	51
Christmas Log	52

Global Trails

In Galway the Devil is on a Bike	54
The Man with No Face	55
Cruise Liner	57
Cocklers	59
Slave Song	60

Table Football and Other Nonsense

In the Land of Hot Toddies	64
Hallowe'en	66
Fireclown	67
Starlight	69
Too Much Stuff	70
Save the Last Dance for Me	71
Bloody Hopeless	72

Wordsworth's Goggles

Poetry	74
False Summer	75
The Last Wolf	76
Little Egrets	77
Otterman	78

Kazoos and Mirror Balls

Today	80
Sharing Birthdays	81
For Flo	82
For Reuben	82
Wedding Poem for Jamie and Val	83 86
For John and Martin	87

Knowing What to Do

Meadowsweet	88
Stone Graves	89
Evensong	90
Looking for a Princess	91
Fisherman's Arms	92
Wood Pile	93

Coda

Lullaby	97

This book of poems for occasions is dedicated to all my family, particularly **Sue Gill**, brilliant wife and editor.

My thanks also to Pat Belshaw, Peter Croskery, Dan Fox, Hannah Fox, John Robinson and especially Clive Tempest for editorial advice and proof reading.

Thanks to Tim Fleming and Pete Moser for setting the songs to music.

Profane and Sacred

Gate

Here is a new gate. Chunky,
no nonsense sentinel framing the gap
between the lane and the bank
where the wild garlic grows.
Unlike the view from the house
it signals to the West,
where behind clumps of mud-dragged cattle
the evening sun takes your breath away.

We look East
preferring a morning house for each new day
to rise behind the silhouette
of the dawn thrush.
We encompass the sun rolling round the Bay,
snookering Morecambe on the horizon.
Sometimes mist obliterates this painted world
whispering to us of the limitless drop behind.

Between the boundary gate and the changing
scenery we cosset and embellish our ark.
Between elder and cherry tree
we draw winter curtains, open summer doors,
surprise ourselves with bones and shells
to decorate our raft with memory
and the fragile belief of belonging.

I have seen paintings of blue gates
opening to the West
where souls helter-skelter
down chutes of no return.

On the still sills of windows
hedgerow bouquets in peasant jugs
are frothy with sunlit autumns.

Inside we pretend that time stands still.

Outside the sun boots you up the arse
and the gate creaks.

Half Moon Bay

There was a purpose about Half Moon Bay.
A headland.
An orientation.
A rise and fall.
Curved walls.
Selected cobblestones.
An understanding of time and tide,
of what will be revealed at the bend of the moon.
The balance of shingle and bladderwrack
where mussels cling and sewage falls.

Steps, very old, lead to
dripping woods.
Here in the cave of imagined hermits
roots knuckle deep
and bottles, needles and silver foil
are embedded in dank mud.
A place to lie in litter,
lost in an alcoholic crawl of worms.

No time-worn priest remains
to love or mulch this flesh.
Bury me with an airline pillow.
Inflated.
What does it matter?

Come in Noah

When shingle floods in a foul tide
decimating antique guitars and photo albums
filling each orifice and flute hole
with stinking mud

when removal men
with Stanley knives
are slicing Chinese carpets
and you may not get insurance,
then call for Noah.

Noah will pluck a shrimp from a camel's ear.
Noah will sprinkle myrrh on the udder of a goat.

The dove is more uncertain though.
She flew off without a brolly.
Took refuge in a cellar bar
and stuffed herself with olives.

Washed Up

When the power failed
Mrs Lighthouse Keeper
took to whisky.
She threw away the message bottles.
Always had done,
always would.
Except for one.

The one that she kept
stood in a niche
by the porthole of dawn
containing an acorn bursting into leaf.

No words.
No sentimental garbage.
Just an acorn.
Something to wait for.

Worth a double scotch.

Superstore

Over 60s' Shopping Day at B&Q.
Wednesdays 10% off.

In the Cathedral of too much choice
galaxies of tools dangle
like waxy appendages.

Jubilee clips only come in packets of 20.

Until an hydraulic angel
(dreaming of Saturday night)
descends to Trolley Central,
where, despite the rattle of excommunication,
as my plastic fails at the checkout,
she finds a pack of 2 and
takes old money.

Yellow Ducks

At the Hospice Garden Party
ladies with tombolas and chocolate muffins
raise funds for water beds and soft pyjamas.

Fluorescent banners tug and flap,
shadowing the triple glazing of
windows double locked.
All patients kept inside.

One,
his face bluebottle blue,
is wheeled to the window
next to pink pot pourris
and radiators too hot to touch.

A hundred plastic ducks
with a hundred numbered bottoms
are flung into the river.
All patients kept inside.

In a whipping wind
we anchor flags with sticks and stones.

Getting Old
Song

She doesn't say she is
the oldest person in the world.

When you speak
she knows her name.
She'll say yes or no or laugh.

She doesn't say she has
lived alone in three world wars.

When you speak
she asks your name.
She'll say yes or no or laugh.

She doesn't say she is
the oldest person in the world.

She bakes new
bread every day.
Freshly baked for your return.

She bakes new bread every day.
Makes sure it doesn't burn.

Farewell Party for Dr P.

Nurses in high time stilettos
circle handbags until dawn,
clinking juice and rattling banter,
obliterating
silent processions and rubber wheels.

Put your whole self in,
Howdie Horsie Cowgirls.
Rock the scented sports club.
Rip down the word retirement.
Burst balloons
lipsticked with luck.
Just grab
the nearest dick
and dance like fuck.

Urn

At Bean Well
where the schooners came for fresh water
a plastic urn from the crem
is kicking around in soggy watercress.

No label, just glue
where the name once was.

Tossed up on the tide
with a missing lid
it's the usual colour of brown sauce.

On the side in felt pen:
"I will always love you
and miss you so much.
Your big Sis xx"

Maybe the ashes are in the shingle,
or blown grey into the dunes
where the black rooks gossip?

Fancy would have them land in a heronry,
or drift on a liner
to the waltzing antipodes.

The urn is under our eaves.
Its job done.

Funerals

In the last three years over a dozen of our friends and colleagues have died.

Most of these poems were read at their funerals or memorial services. Many of them worked with Welfare State International and were eccentric and wonderful inventors, performance artists, poets and dreamers.

The Age of Wisdom

The only wisdom that comes
is coping when your friends die.

The phone rings.
A recurring bleep of disconnection.
Voice mail lingers.
Pen hovering before the crossing out.

Kept awake
by relentless snapshots
of impossible nostalgia.
A drip of rain at 5 am
tapping out
disappointment rather than fear.

Always the unresolved
and the stupid failure to celebrate
what might have been
or in fact was.

Apple blossom blowing unnoticed.
A penknife not returned.
The inscription mislaid.

Diz Willis

There are a thousand stories.
He was the great God Pan.
Trucking with goats in an ancient transit van.
He took them into tea shops;
they drank whisky from a can.
There are a thousand stories
of his giant frying pan.
He cooked rabbits with black pudding in a flan
then served it in a car park
with the wine of Caliban.
He told a thousand stories
with wit and surreal bite.
Wild pigeons flew in Norfolk.
Giants danced at night
performing to the world
in distinctive holey tights.
Incredible are the tales
of this telephoning hoaxer.
International operators fell to his encroaches.
"My brother has a shoe shop in Macedonia.
 It's urgent please to tell him
his eggs are boiling over."

So DIZ DEVIL,
Human goat, comic chaotic anti-dote,
thank you.
May your memories
keep rocking all our boats.

Midnight Mechanics
For Greville

I know at times he could whinge
and wasn't always himself,
but when it came to making things
Greville was second to none.
He made a shoal of piranha fish in metal
to devour an old folks home.
He made a juke box sphinx on
the boot of a family car.
In Vancouver under Route 66
he made the Limping Horse of History.
Then the burning skull of Mirrorman
which strimmed the only lawn in Expo '86.

Wiper motors, magnets and mirror balls
were as cig papers in his dexterity.
Subverting acrobatic bedsprings
he giggled like a piston engine primed on meths.
Yet when it came to accolades
Greville preferred none at all.
He was happy with whisky
and the laughing company
of midnight mechanics
wiring oily batteries to the Milky Way.
This time there was no explosion.
He died of a heart attack
in bed on Sunday morning.
Unpredictable as ever.

Bells
For Peter Feversham

We could hear them in the bread shop.
In the newsagent and the café loo.
They rang for hours over cobbles
and lines of mourners too.
They boomed out,
boomed out over estate and dale,
clunking English discord on the wild wood trail.
Bikers, buses, walkers all
held awhile to heed
the swinging anvil call:
His Lordship is dead.
Dead. Dead. Dead.
His Lordship is dead is dead.
Dead. Dead. Dead.

We came from miles.
Filled the aisles and bleached marquees
perched 'tween graves and sinewed trees.
For the Lord was dead.
To fill columns of The Times
(or was it Yorkshire Life?)
we must be on a list.
A wrinkly usher with a biro tottered by the porch
seeking names for posterity and Court.
Her fingers shook.
Her notebook fell.
I'm up since milking.
These bells are hell.

Max

Max is dead. Sorry to be blunt.
He wasn't one for words.
He worked with his hands.
Engineer, fitter, mechanic, builder, driver,
collector of vans, wandering welder, man with
trailer, occasional plumber, father and generous
friend. Our last conversation concerned
waterproofing cement, windmills, batteries and
emergency power.

He fixed our water
when no one else would or could.
Straddling a bronco digger,
a boy with a Tonka toy,
he hurled it at the trench
till the water had to flow.
The flood came down the lane.
Nearly burst the drain.
And the overflow was waterlogged again
and then again.
"Too much pressure," shouted Max
as he crawled beneath the boiler.
Then he fixed it fast and
undercharged us for the valves.

I imagine him now MIG welding still.
Fixing storms to fall in reservoirs.
Channelling whirlpools.
Without the pressure.

Captain Fantastic

For Richard's funeral in the crem
the crucifix has been removed.

Women with accumulations of rouge
and men in Richard-a-Like lumberjack shirts
are gathered early.

The central heating kicks in
and the polished oak pongs.

Blunt on rollers
the white cardboard coffin
is laid with clean beer mats
inscribed with felt pens.

"You owe me a pint."
" I'll see you Richard."
" The next one's on me."

As his bike is wheeled up the aisle
a pannier of stories is released.

He went camping but forgot the tent.
We all drove to Spain.
He hitch hiked and got there first.
He was starkers when he tackled that wild boar
with a harpoon he bought at Oxfam.
Starkers and without a tent as well.

No idea he could run like that.

Five Poems for Boris
Boris co-directed Welfare State International for 12 years.

ONE

I had always imagined you would end your days in Dragon Fire,
or fall without sandwiches from the North Face of the Eiger.
However a motor mower in the sun is not bad.
Not so heroic
but practical as usual.

TWO

We were at the Teachers' Conference
when you nailed the carcass of a goat
to the polystyrene ceiling.
There was blood on the carpet
and education was never quite the same.

THREE

Your Northumberland Pipes
have gone to Australia,
wrapped in antique leather,
polished with your DNA,
warmed with your voice.
They will pour mellifluous nectar
into the drought of the new world.

FOUR

You are to be buried in your wood.
In the next aeons
when determined hunters gather on hilltops
above the waves
in your forest
they will hear you singing.
See the prow bones of your skull
while their
grandchildren listen too.

FIVE

Before we quarrelled,
God knows why,
we promised we would sup
fine Malt on the xylophone of zimmer frames,
laughing with nostalgia at the chaos we had
caused.
Well Boris I am not laughing now.
But I am not weeping either.
I loved you too much to forget the beauty you
brought to so many
and the fun we had together.
Voyage on you old bugger.

Arthur

Beaked nose.
Thin skin.
No weight.
Arthur is becoming a bird.
Dying men do.
As the train passes over the marsh
to the factory on the island
Arthur remembers swallows
returning to that place.
Remembers mirrors on poles
to watch them feeding.
Of the same swallows always returning
and the managers smashing their nests.

Twelfth of May 2010

Arthur died last night.
Just after the Archers.
They all said it wasn't fair.
His throat stretching for air.
No one should have to die like that.
Last night the political limbo ended in a deal.
They all said they wanted to be fair.
We lit two white candles.
One for Arthur. One for Mary.
Wax poured over the edge
in a slipstream shroud.
One wrinkled and translucent.
The other held still and clear.

View

In between the hail and the grey
a rising corrugation of sea water
comes juddering
up river.
The sunset is the same.
The same view we painted on her coffin.
The view she saw coming home.

Waiting for the Light
*For Mick who was, long ago, the best man at
our wedding. A fine teacher and a good artist.*

In the early hours
he copied Masaccio's
Expulsion from Eden.

Again and again until their luminous flesh
danced free
of the glare of the Red Angel.

In the late morning
he lies dead in the stale church.
Ushers crow round his veneered coffin,
continuing to smear darkness
into the last shaft
of God's light.

Mermaids over Arran

Jude disliked flowers cut to size.
She had no time for roses trapped in planters.
She hated pavement cherry trees, fluffed up to
bloom in May.

"Do not muck about with Nature," Jude said.

And practised what she preached,
with wellies,
pruning shears
and a vision that held us all.

Many children in the City
may thank her for enchantment
in their wilderness of dreams.

Many punters walking home
hear a xylophone of rain
under her monumental trees.

And now from her peaceful resting place
in a field of uncut flowers,
where the trees hold hands with the sky,
she sees mermaids over Arran.

There in the randomness of roots
our bulbs will flash their skirts,
to welcome in the Spring.

In Memory of Val

Yesterday a riderless horse on the beach,
a bat flittering in the light of day
and cherry leaves falling early.
Let's be rational.
The saddle was slack.
The bat smelled garlic on the barbecue
and climate change has warmed the wind.
Let's be rational.
The garden fire we lit last night has gone out.
That glimmer is merely the solar lamp from
some while back.

Some while back
you were cycling from Lands End
to John O' Groats
and jogging and singing and
teaching for 30 years,
inspiring generations of children hard to reach.
"Bit of a racy wheelchair you've got there Val,"
I quipped, on the way to that band gig.
I remember we all dined
on prawns in candlelight,
your cheekbones pink with skull -like beauty.

Not long back
before the clamour took our ears away.
Being rational.
The cancer had no apparent reason.

Yet you have left us with so much.

Bryan, Tamsin, Hannah, Olivia and Freya
for a start.
And scores of children who can now add up.

Above all such caring for others
in your half-year's dying.

May I be able to die with such dignity.

Thank you Val.

Adrian
I love you Adrian Mitchell because 20 years ago you wrote a poem for my daughter Hannah.

Happy Breakfast Hannah
On your 18th Birthday.

Today you sit down for a proper breakfast.
Yesterday you were seventeen,
on the Sunny Side of the Century
arranged for ukulele and spotty pyjamas.

The day before yesterday you were twelve.
All woolly hat, armfuls of homework,
the largest eyes in the known world.
And sudden laughter beside a lake.

The day before that you were six and a bit
in enormous boots and a housewife hat
chasing the vicar with your deadly gamp.

And the day before that, eighteen years ago,
the midwife said:
"This one's been here before,"
as you came up really bright into the light.

And I wish you a house in a wood
within the sighing of the sea.
Animals around your feet.
And the music of peacetime
to dance your own dance.

And all the love in the world, lovely Hannah
as you came up bright into the light.

I love you Adrian Mitchell
because it all came true.
The wood sings with owls.
The house dances with children.
Ginger cats chase
lusty chickens up farmyard frontiers
while family bonfires entwine over the sighing
Irish Sea so near.

I love you Adrian Mitchell
because in all your lovely
gifts you drew a dog
or a wiry elephant dreaming peace.

I love you Adrian Mitchell because
You stomped out great songs for our shows.
Titanic, King Real and Lancelot Quail,
Uppendown Mooney and On the Loose.
Fiery anthems that rolled on coasters of truth.

I love you Adrian Mitchell because as we sang
that night with Albert Hunt
the piano stood up, the black notes fell
and all the guns in the world burned in Hell.

You squeezed our guts
and cracked the capitalist juggernuts.

And

I have proof you used a rhyming dictionary.

I love you Adrian Mitchell
because you illuminate the shadows.

In the stuttering night
when the moon has failed to rise
or "packed her bags"
as you wrote for our Tales for a Winter's Night,
I need poetry bright as sparklers
and sharp as a West Coast malt.

I need verse
free of any jackets of dust.
I need Orpheus.
I need wild songs.

I need that Sunny Side.
I need poetic pillars of fresh sea salt.
So when I read your poems Adrian
and I hear your voice,
you help me ride the nightmare.

Adrian Mitchell.

Thank you.

A Question of Time

Hollow

Some days feel hollow.
Not too many.
When the wheedling of lambs
turns to braying.
When gulls spindrift shrieking
and our regular old crow,
ragged on a north east gust,
loses the straw from its beak;
then the day can be hollow.
For age mounts remorselessly,
as the skin of each hour
gathers prophetically
puckering thin into a slack tide.

Age must chew over the failed increments
of a reduced pension.
Age must speak reluctantly
with stiff fingers on yellowed keyboards.
Kick the sulky armchair.
Light the fire.
Hump wood and tend sparks until
old cuttings are burnt
and the chill ghost slithers off
to a tamed mist.
Seek out freshly ground hollows
to unearth some wayward sprig of chance
for tossing up to that salivating crow.

On the Edge of a Heaving Tide

Inside the Beach House
Sunday morning 20th February 2000.
Two ginger wrens
patrol for earwigs in our beams.

Ignoring the snoring duvet of the one eyed poet
they scrimp through a hairline crack,
popping to the beach
to take refuge in a blackthorn pile
on the edge of a heaving tide.

Inside the Beach House
Sunday evening after dinner
knock at the door
and a near full moon behind the cloud.
"It's only us."

In from the rain.
Snuggling by the stove
nestling in the white arm chair,
you say simply:
"We have something to tell you -

"I - well, we - are going to have a baby."

Then the party starts.

Under constellations of sea-washed confetti
and wild swans honking,
an upturned lantern boat
with it's golden aura
bursts ribs on the evening tide.

The terracotta dove,
sedate on its block of resinous larch,
goes broody as a Moroccan prune
cooing a sexy samba for songbirds
stepping high on their feather xylophone.

Meanwhile in the kitchen
a hundred pink-headed matches
blushing like boys fall into fabulous chaos,
imagining a forest fire bent daft in the gale,
dreaming of girlish saplings and spring ships.

The wrens are dancing too.
Squeezing in and out of their special place
in a pokey tango,
'til two tiny feathers spiral over the mezzanine
settling, fingers crossed in surprise,
nestling on the warm hearth below.

On the edge of a heaving tide.

Frame Raising
Poem for the Beach House Topping Out Ceremony.

The skeleton of the building
holds its ribs steady,
ready
for fleshing out.

We tore down
heaps of neglect.
Mouldy wallpaper
and sour plaster
embedded
with cloudy sentiments.

We revealed foundations.
Dug tunnels.
Flattened rats.
Ripped boards.
Pulled nails.
Cut brambles.
Humped cement.
Carted larch
and
calculated angles.

Above, the world slipstreams by.
Below, the sea rips away remaining clutter.

A Question of Time

Today 27 November 2008 is Dan's 40th.
A wild wind is hugging the house.
We can't grasp the journeying of the years.
So where did the time go?
This year's crab apple jelly took five hours:

Hour One: Collecting

The old tree is embedded in a cliff of grey clay.
A myriad of crab apples lie on a rooty bank.
Some hidden in mud and thorns.
Harvesting is spiky and slippery.
Each apple unique.
Large or small, yellow or green, bruised or clean.
Before the light goes
we have a bucket full.

Hour Two: Washing

In our pearly apple bowl
fronds of grass and crispy leaves are entwined.
Clay is smeared on the yellow and green.
Weals disfigure flesh,
ancient barnacles from a rusty planet.

A few are rotten as prunes.
Some soft as cushions.
My hands are cold so I add water from the kettle
and rinse and rinse
our plenitude.

Hour Three: Slicing

They have to be quartered.
Green to white. White to brown. Pod to seed.
Each core a different tale.
A moon. A smile. A kidney spare.
The kitchen knife is sharp as they come.
Chop chopping on wood
obliterating girdle gossip on Woman's Hour.

Hour Four: Cooking - 1

Take a large heavy-bottomed pan.
Boil all fiercely - pips and stalks and skins.
Squeeze the ragbag pulp through muslin or
plastic sieve.
Push it and thrust and scrape it through
'til the gold of the pulp runs pure.
Then,
weigh and balance
with equal amount of sugar.

Hour Five: Cooking - 2

Pause.
Add the sugar to the pulp.
Pause.
On top, the sugar waits,
luminous as frost on a honey beach.
Pause.
Stir slowly. Clockwise. Timewise.

Savour the stirring
before the second boiling begins.

Then
the bubbling is remorseless.
Blister heat in the cauldron,
syrup transforming crimson.
Coagulating.
Apple alchemy is complete.
The boiling is still.
The sun is locked.

Cool slabs of Crab Apple Cheese are ready.

"The Ultimate Abode of the Just"
Definition of Paradise in the Oxford Compact English Dictionary.
For Sue Gill

We could be on another beach
barbecuing fish,
sipping coconut delights
from a turquoise dish.

We could be on an island
tanning on a deck,
reading old whodunits
scuba diving wrecks.

No.
Paradise is your old back in the bath
which candlelight makes young.

It is mulling wine
after trekking in blinding sleet.

A heron watches us.
Oystercatchers chunter,
for the sea has turned to ice.

Paradise is winter fire,
burning logs we stacked
in sweat
in summer.

Lugworms

The two of us step lightly on immense sand,
crunching a flat iron of eternity between
tide fall and tide rise
sun fall and moon rise.
mesmerised by runic cracks
spreading along the dry beach
we spot codes of love.

We know
the lurking sea,
slithering into scissory gullies,
could outflank us;
making us swim for it
or drown in wool and leather.

Across the bay
the sun glows on a white hotel
small as a burning cinder,
small as lugworms underfoot.

Out here
their minuscule cairns radiate
through shadowland
sculpting a million markers
to anthill moon.
We orbit arm in arm
leaning into an ellipse,
returning home before definition goes.

There will be Forever Herrings

Another day fishing.
Big fresh herrings to gut and barbecue.

As the children fall asleep
we put their minnows back
and paddle to the centre of the easeful bay
where mist and mountains mingle pink.

Above the mist
on the curvature of the forest rim
a randy moon cocks a snook
at our canoe.

As well-worn geese honk away
and the first star twinkles on fishy scales

it seems
this evening

that nothing really changes
and there will be forever herrings.

Curlew

The curlew's head is clawed with flies.
No longer a smear, feathered umber
on the tar post.
Just bones picked clean.

Reuben found the carcass way out in the Bay
and carried it home for Grandad.
Weighing more than a bag of spuds
with one leg broken it stank of guts.

We cut off its head.
The beak curved long for rooting in mud.
Now with surgeon perfection
we add it to our skull collection.

Nana's Dance

On the shore
evening shadows are watercolour violet.
On the shore
each cranny is filled with the sparkle of birds.
From the shore,
from the sticky beach,
Rosa is breakwater dancing away.
Unflinching.
Knee high.

Getting smaller.

You follow on.
Spiralling into
a certain dance of age.

Christmas Log

The tide line of the old year
is blocked with withered leaves.
In our shack
a gale force intrusion
tangles red ribbons
of Christmas cards stapled in haste.

These dangling blood lines
hold urgent information.

Ted died.
Lewis is autistic.
Are you grandparents yet?

Stem the draught.

Global Trails

In Galway the Devil is on a Bike
For Noeline

Certainty is a wise crocodile
 carrying her babies in fierce teeth.

Certainty is a chocolate ballroom in the sky
where traffic wardens penalize marshmallows.

Certainty is knowing your gears,
remembering bruise cream for your arse
and checking your panniers at dawn.

Certainty is being aware of the white hare
in your back wheel,
of the stray strap flapping in the wind.
Loose chippings, wet tar,
and the slip-stream of 4 x 4s.

Blokes can always sit on a rock in the sun,
eating fruitcake from Swinford,
dreaming of tits and poetry
at the end of the runway.

Within yellow lines.

The Man with No Face
*A song from Longline, the Carnival Opera
WSI's last show.*

I am the man you never see,
the one behind the door.
I control the programme
of the air waves in the sky.
I have no face.
I am the faceless nightmare
in your dreams.

When you buy into roulette
I am the croupier who figures
the hidden trigger.

When you binge into the night
I am the brewer who powers
the spirits of happy hour.

When you climb the prison wire
I am the agent who governs
cyanide in the ovens.

When the poor grovel in the ditch
I am the government that bent
the fairest trade agreement.

When the hidden grave is found
I am the dealer in machetes
who put the bodies in the dirt.

When the minaret is bombed
I am the profiteer who sold
sweet Kalashnikovs for gold.

I am the man you never see,
the one behind the door.
I control the programme
of the air waves in the sky.

Cruise Liner
Cabaret chorus from Longline, the Carnival Opera.

From our window we can see
the curving of the world,
an indigo horizon in the sand.
A liner is cruising,
a smoke stack appears,
port holes trail glow-worms galore.

Here is a pile of temptation.
I want an authentic fiddle
to hang on the wall of my bar.
I need St Patrick in portico marble for my
dying mum's front door.
Transport me to the beach and the rum,
to riches beyond
my own doorstep of shifting sand.

Oh Cruise Liner,
Cruise Liner of fun,
your chapel is warmed with a terminal sun.
Lifebelt halos guarantee heaven.

My haven.
My haven.

Come into my ballroom chants
the Captain of the ship.

Or is it the Holy Ghost, St Anchovy on the Sick?

Come in.
Come in.

The anchorite intones.
We need your souls and you need us.
So are the needy cloned.

In the wheelhouse chamber bankers gamble
with our gold,
dealing slaves for dynamite and coffee beans
twice sold.

Bid more.
Bid more.

The Central Bank declares.
The engine of this Ship of State
is fuelled with your shares.
In the hold beneath the water
a little secret hides.
A hanger full of warheads and propaganda lies.

Stand up.
Stand up.

The Government decrees.
You have the choice to buy our goods
or be targets when we please.

Cocklers
On 5th February 2004 in Morecambe Bay 23 migrant Chinese workers were drowned while gathering cockles.

With the regularity of wrapped bandages
tides sweep grey across the sands.

Flotsam and jetsam tossed to the edge
of a living or a drowning.

Cockles proliferate
sucking plankton.
Spiralling in those galactic seedings
noted by astrophysicists and fishermen.

Today the refrigerated truck from Spain
waits.

Inscribed on its empty metal side,
the Jesus logo
is a bleeding heart.
Not unlike a cockle.
His finger points
to paella in Benidorm.

Slave Song

Song from Longline, the Carnival Opera, about a young slave known as Sambo who died in 1736 on the east side of Morecambe Bay. His grave may still be visited at Sunderland Point. The song is also about 'surplus' child labourers, lured to their deaths near Ulverston.

If you are no longer a child you are dead.
If you no longer hear the sound of the air
ripped by the wings of a bird you are dead.
If you no longer dream of building piers
and climbing
ashen stones to the custard moon,
you are dead.

I was put outside the tribe.
Buried low in a field of poppies instead
of resting in the tomb of the churchyard dead.

I was put in a place of children
who bring strips of taffeta
to tie their dreams on a tree of souls.

Where teddy bears and pepsi tins
and humbug stones
flag the shape of innocence
in childhood snapshots round my grave.

I was put inside a stone shed
chained fast to a loom of metal instead
of following herons overhead.
I was put in a zone of quicksand
empty picnic hampers to float my limbs
on the rising tide.
Feeling sand between your toes you are alive.

Fish wriggle underfoot, you are alive.
Held by a song which whispers in the reeds.

Where we still sing.

If all the children on the earth
could dance with us today
sharing our tears in their wide poppy eyes.
Tears of dreams of childhood.

Where we still sing.

Our sad ghosts remain
lamenting on the ebb tide.
Knowing today beneath satellite eyes
children die in thousands.

Table Football and
Other Nonsense

In the Land of Hot Toddies

The talent is going for make believe.

Before Santa has time to drink his sherry
an unwanted table football game,
dumped in the barn,
is disassembled
to get it through the kitchen door.

Reassembled for
Warthogs versus Black Ants
the finale is raucously imminent.

Rosa, rising eight, tootles Match of the Day
on a half eaten pear
miming to her uncle hiding under the table
who is playing a found trumpet
for the first time.

A bundle of kitten - was it a kitten ?
- darts under our feet.

First deaths can be remembered
although the buried bones
of baby hedgehog are forgotten.

The fox got the chickens
but we got some more.
Supermarket eggs
have no mud or feathers

And we just ate Thunder and Lightning.
Their crackled pig thighs
spluttering from the oven
served with apple chutney and pickled onions.

Both condiments the colour of oaked prayers.

There's a new doll's house too
and a new secondhand bike with proper gears.

But there's a family footie game to get on with.

To fulfil with generous leaping.

Where spinning is cheating.

And nobody minds at all.

Hallowe'en

Droves of luminous warts
are peering through our front door.
Frankenstein all of five
wobbles between trick and treat.
His mother whispers:
"£1 is too much.
Go for the barley sugar."
Fact is,
backlit wrinklies,
podgy
oily
huge
in marshmallow cardigans,
glowing like pumpkins with brandy snap teeth
ARE
monsters.

Fireclown

Fireclown's in the garden.
Keep your mother out of sight.
A painted beast that smells of yeast
is looking in our window.
Phone the Council.
Phone the Health.
Phone the Mortgage.
Phone the Telly
and the Official Speaking Clock.

He might empty slops on the daisies on our lawn.
He might steal our babies
in the hours before dawn.
He might drive our car over cliffs in the night.
He might bang a drum and give us all a fright.

Now Fireclown's in my dreams
nothing seems quite right.

His tongue is spiced with reptile juice,
his ribs with fossil scales.
His megalithic spine is ringed
with fins of southern whales.

He burns the regimented sinews
in the cod roes of my brain.
He burns the book-rack history
of the segments in my back.

He burns the pearly anchors
on the twin set of my wife.

Fireclown's in the garden.
Keep your mother out of sight.
Fireclown's in the garden.
Now nothing isn't right.

Starlight
Australia

Under this toe-nail of a moon,
starlight.
Black mountains carved with raggedy totems
of emu and kangaroo
spill blood dust and honey dreaming
in scarred circles.

I, a mere speck,
dally in a swag
on the inner tube of the lower rim
of the Milky Way.

A vast glitter wheel
marks the spokes of night
while the hot wind
tugs the rubber valves of my toes.

I stare.
Looking for the bike pump man.

Too Much Stuff
Australia

Too much stuff they shouted
as they packed the van with more.
We'll need a parasol.
It could be an umbrella.
The goose will go inside the cardboard box.
You've forgotten the goanna.
And do we really need
that pink lounge any more?
What about the paperweight
that Auntie gave to me?
It's inside the colander, inside the pan,
in the electric cooker.
Where's the portable TV?
It's with the woolly panda.
No, it's in the box marked "spare"
labelled "in case of need".
We'll need another suitcase
for the bags we can't get in
and a bag for all the plastic things
recycled from the bin.
Christ! I've forgotten the spaghetti.
I'm giving it to Pat. What?
Don't say what to me.
What do you mean don't say what?
Just what are you trying to say?

I'm trying to say let's stuff it. What?
Burn the bloody lot. What? What!

Save the Last Dance for Me

When you are old
the dance floor still reflects
your tapping feet
and men at bars still ogle.

Give us the Sunny Side of the Street.
And repeat.
And repeat.
Until our toes squeeze through
the honky-tonk cracks of
the ballroom in the sky.
And repeat.
And repeat.

Bloody Hopeless
For my daughter Hannah - artist, performer, film and theatre maker.

You hid your first man
in the attic for several months.
But your first car was more up front.
I who read texts on women's rituals
and period things
missed your first car.

Three years' student debt gone deeper.
A roof rack, for surfboards, rather wide.
You up all night
shaping the inside
with my best wood.
A wondrous diesel Bedford Astra B Reg.
Deep red.
Shiny, streamlined, burnished and bountiful.

First trip. Breaks down.
Your mother tows you in at dawn,
her clothesline snapping seven times.

The AA man chimes in.
"Christ!" he says,
"what did you pay for this?"

Wordsworth's Goggles

Poetry

The trouble with writing poetry
is that you end up with poetry.
Perfectly honed maybe,
balanced and literate.
Not too many adjectives of course,
distilled, predictable
and dull.

Ditch water is never dull.
When you think you have nipped
the ripples and the sunlight
into a grown up synthesis
some water boatman comes rowing in.
Or a dead stump from an incompetent abattoir
rises leering to the surface.

False Summer

The raggedy leaves on the cherry tree,
transparent scrotums of a delayed autumn,
will not fall.

The sloes are too fat
even for the stubby greenfinch.

Something is afoot.

The Bay is silting up.
Hippo Rock is under sand
and Oak Tree Horse has lost its seesaw branch
under a shingle pile.

We lunch with bare feet on a blistered deck,
while, in slits of rootless earth,
children, stiff with starvation,
raise boneyard fingers in a dust of accusation.

The Last Wolf
*Thought to have been killed on Humphrey
Head, a finger of land that points into
Morecambe Bay opposite the Beach House.*

After the Crusades he
killed the last wolf in England.
"One infidel is as good as another."

So,
in romantic paradise
wilderness was anaesthetized.

Children acquired Wordsworth goggles
lest blackthorns scrape their eyes,
while Nature was reduced
to television size.

Yet ghost prints are on our lawn
and wilderness is in the wood,
lurking in coughing fits of blood.

Little Egrets

A million women in feathered hats
are waltzing with aplomb,
preening coronets and curlicues
in ballrooms nearly gone.

Paint is curling damp
over cherubs' faded wings,
chariots wait with bullets,
arrows and lead-filled slings.

Once upon a morning
egrets were the fashion.
Tangled up in millinery,
monied to extinction.

Now sucked in by global warming,
exotic, in reeds once more.
Dashing the white pageant
in dew lights by the shore.

Excuse me it's my foxtrot.
Is the orchestra to hand?
Come swing with me and Eurydice
in diadems of sand.

Otterman

For the third relentless year
the snow is hard as armour.
A baleful warrior waiting.

Otterman is limping up the lane.
Sea-heavy logs dragging behind.
His twisted beast boots
printed in the snow
are angled against the flow.

Behind, his river is frozen.
The forest is broken.
And the blizzard
has wiped
his remains.

Kazoos and Mirror Balls

Today
For Rowan's first birthday

Today your first clocks back day.
Today your first drum kit.
Today your first tumble in autumn leaves.
Already you can clap,
know the difference between a Knock-Kneed
Elephant and a Woolly Kangaroo.
And you can find the Joey Baby too.
From the big box
you pull your own leaves of white tissue paper.
So many tiny flags
sailing and tumbling
tumbling and sailing high
through these surprising days of darkness.
Dancing, doubtless, to the harbour
of your first birthday.

Sharing Birthdays
For Rowan's second birthday

In the warm
our game is hide and seek.
Peekaboo with the iron weight
behind the kitchen door.
Seventy years between us.
Sagittarians of the same breath
blowing out our runway of candles
firm on the chocolate cake.
Laughing eyes.
Eyes.
Eyes through smouldering wicks.
First you see us then you don't.
Solid baubles on the dropping tree
glimmering with repeated light.

For Flo

Flo is four.
In between the stars and the yurts
the tribe gathers once more.
On the screen the years dissolve
in a kaleidoscope of joy.
In the garden the old scarecrow,
still in his pyjamas,
sighs to see those runner beans
doing the twist again.

For Reuben
Message on his birthday card.

When a boy is 10
he's gone into double figures.
1 is the single little man. 0 is the world ahead.
At ten this boy can roll the world,
sail round it in a skimming Hawk.
Fly with super lenses to steer above the waves.
The Black Ant Club holds the earth
with a football at the centre.
At swimming he's the tops.
Climbing trees and feeding pigs
and making prints and boiling skulls.

Reuben never stops. Reuben is no fool.
In fact... he's rather **COOL**

Wedding Poem for Jamie and Val

Jamie and Val just got married.
Rumour resounds round the Dales;
an MC, three vicars, a Citroen carriage
and wedding rings that blew off in the gales.

This Christian deed was put in a frame
by hench women and two best men.
By gum, yon chapel at t 'end of our lane
ell not see owt like this agaenn.

On Stag night we went for a curry.
Jamie was very soon starkers.
Swopped his wedding suit (and money)
for a vindaloo magic carpet.

He set sail flushed as houses,
in a spiral over Halifax.
Cows looked up from chewing grass
oops, Moon's not wearing trousers.

After a goodly while he came down to earth
on the porch of number eight.
Val came out, observed his girth,
shrieked: "You'll have to wait."

So once our lovers are on Eurostar
on their Spanish honeymoon
a thousand gherkins in tapas bar
will rattle all afternoon.

Val and Jamie are in Barcelona
famed for its art and its nuts.
"I know you can be a bit of a loner," says Val,
" but I love you and your ... garden huts."

" I've heard Gaudi was a building wag," says
Jamie, " but his Cathedral isn't finished."
So he takes a trowel from his big tool bag
and downs a can of spinach.

Then it's up with ladders at crack of dawn
and humping cement in the sun.
Diggers and dumpers all night 'til morn.
No honeymoon was ever such fun.

Just one more fag and one more beer
Cathedral towers are now complete.
Jamie cheers from the final tier.
Barcelona and Flushhouse are both reel reet.

Seeing Jamie, handy man, on a scaffold so high
Val iPods her very own choir.
So sweet anthems rebound in the sky.
Good old Gaudi. Great Balls of Fire.

Returning to earth at number eight
they wonder was it just a sweet dream?
"Did we together on our first Spanish date
finish those spires in a head of steam?"

"Of course," says Jamie,"it's built at last, 'cos
English lovers do it reet fast."

"It was a gas," says Val, "and we had a ball.
But what I love Jamie, is really
the Cathedral will NEVER be finished at all."

For John and Martin

Here comes the biggest mirror ball there ever was in a crate that's even bigger. It's here to celebrate the partnership of John and Martin. Outside labelled "Civil Ceremony" inside clearly:

Wedding

It took 25 years to dismantle the packing. There was a time when mirrors were closed or smashed. And even faint reflections were smeared out of existence.

Today's wedding invitation is open. A graphic patchwork of photos: parents, dogs, and childhoods neat and tidy, Michelangelo's David, a fountain rising and a crimson rose surprised. On cue the mirror ball spins, sprinkling a Busby Berkeley moment while roman candles burst in galaxies unseen.

> Now you're in the open guys,
> leaving your dry dock.
> 25 years is but a blink.
> The orchestra is tuning up.
> The flight path shortens though.
> So hang on to your mirror balls
> and that antique ticking clock.

Knowing What to Do

Meadowsweet

Seeds of Meadowsweet
unearthed from a Bronze Age grave.

We always placed flowers on the breast.
Always warmed the hill with weeping.
Always knew what to do.

Stone Graves

Seven stone graves,
side by side,
a bit down hill.
Keyholes carved into rock over sea.
Lids gone.
Skeletons gone
to the palaeontologist's shoe-box.

It was only when
you lay down in the grave
that I knew the plot.
There was still room at the end.

Space at your feet for a potted geranium
or a wrapped embryo.
Something the colour of blood and tears
to be swept out to sea on a South West surge.

Evensong

After hop-stepping an excuse me
on the stone slabs of the Nave,
dancing on the lids
blunt with crossed bones and hour glass skulls,
I sit the next one out.

Too close to the old woman
nodding at the bookstall,
her brittle wrists leaning
on veins soft as plums.

I want a postcard
of Lord Longdead
the one with his marble wife
and cringing weepers,
but have no heart
to startle this frail keeper.

Instead I encounter
a mediaeval mason.
His wrists sinewed
from drilling eye sockets.

Our boots have trod his slate
skin thin.
Yet the holes remain,
black as punctuation.

Looking for a Princess
On taking Rosa my granddaughter round St Bavo's Cathedral in Haarlem, Holland.

The Cathedral
behind the secret door
is smelly with incense and half dead coughs.
An oak mastiff
waxen with the sweat of penitents
guards the confessional.
We tip toe along the grinning rims of tombs
skipping up the aisle,
our necks straining
to galleons soaring with their spider crew.

In the organ of golden minarets
cherubs, deaf with Mozart, conga sublime.
A carved princess in hiding tosses mildew
onto balding priests.

She's seen it all before of course,
but this winter
her woodworm's getting worse.

Fisherman's Arms

In the carpark by the pub
next to Cartmel Priory
there is a kerfuffle
in the stream.

Beyond the Volvo and the Porsche
the reflecting stream is tickling
the bark of chestnut trees.

The carved mermaid from the church
from the third misericord
has left her post.
She no longer finds it fitting
to prop up the arse of the Bishop.

She is away with the Green Man.

Hence sherbert in the stream
as frogs and millipedes
drop from high into
our baked alaska ice cream.

Wood Pile

For my son Dan - inventor, musician and sound interventionist.

Today we chainsaw logs together.
Dan looking young
in an orange hard hat.
Me looking old
in a bulbous sweater.

Logs pile up in steady cairn.
Exhaust from the motor ripples along the bark.
Woodlice and worms
cling and scurry in fungoid soil.

A clear wind blows from Magpie Fields,
fresh as ice,
ferrying fumes to the crab apple stump.
Pruned and severed.
Well cropped for winter.

Coda

Lullaby
Song

Hush now baby
hush now baby hush.

Tide's going out.
Tide's going out.

The world's not upside down.
Follow the plough
to the pole star held forever still.

Hush now baby hush.
The world's not upside down,
the world's not upside down.

Lie you down, lie you down and sleep away.
Close your eyes, close your eyes
and leave the day.
May you dream of stars above the bay.

The world's not upside down.
Follow the plough
to the pole star held forever still.

YOU NEVER KNOW is one of a series of books and art works originating from the **Weather Station** project at the Beach House, on the west shore of Morecambe Bay.

The **Weather Station** by John Fox and Sue Gill includes paintings, etchings, short films, enamels, whirlygigs, biodegradable funeral urns, documentary photography and poetry for occasions. In looking at ecology and perception the artists are collaborating with scientists and secular celebrants to seek a template for a way of living which is both creative and sustainable.

Weather Station was made possible through funding from the Arts and Humanities Research Council (AHRC) with John Fox as a Research Fellow in the Creative and Performing Arts at LICA in Lancaster University.

With their arts company **Welfare State International (WSI)** 1968-2006 John Fox and Sue Gill gained a worldwide reputation for originating prototypes of site specific theatre, community celebrations, lantern festivals, installations and new ceremonies for rites of passage.

Their new company **Dead Good Guides** picks up where **WSI** left off. Fox and Gill are pioneering further prototypes of vernacular art in action. **Publications** available via their website and/or Amazon:

> **Engineers of the Imagination** Methuen
> **Eyes on Stalks** Methuen
> **The Dead Good Funerals Book**
> **The Dead Good Guide to Baby Namings**
> Books for primary age children:
> **Rock in the Sea**
> **Garden in the Sky**
> **Queen of the Sea**
>
> **www.deadgoodguides.com**

blurb.com